Animals That Hatch from Eggs

Children's Science & Nature

BABY PROFESSOR

EDUCATION KIDS

Color the animals.

Turkey

Chicken

Crocodile

Platypus

Peacock

Ostrich

Frog

Penguin

Butterfly

Duck

Turtle

Snake

Spider

Grasshopper

Snail

Bee

Eagle

Gecko

Iguana

Chameleon

Fish

Crab

Lobster

Ant

Echidna

Connect the dots and color the animals.

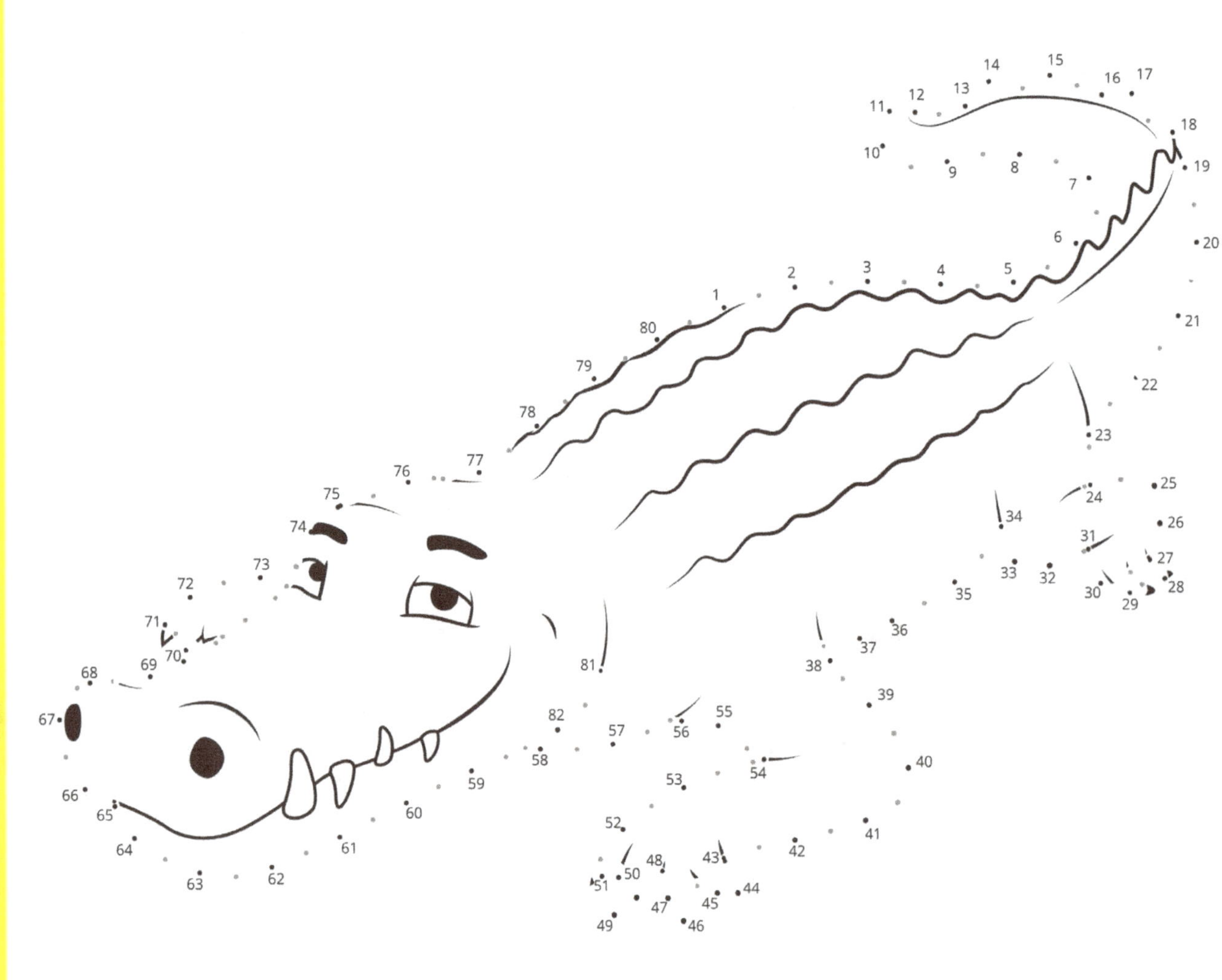

Crocodile

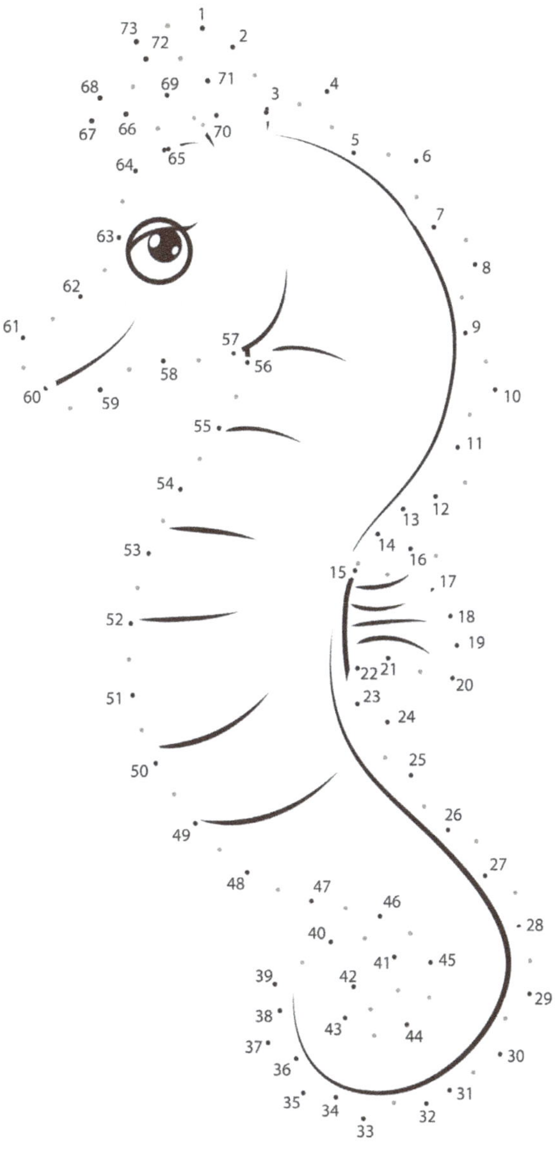

Seahorse

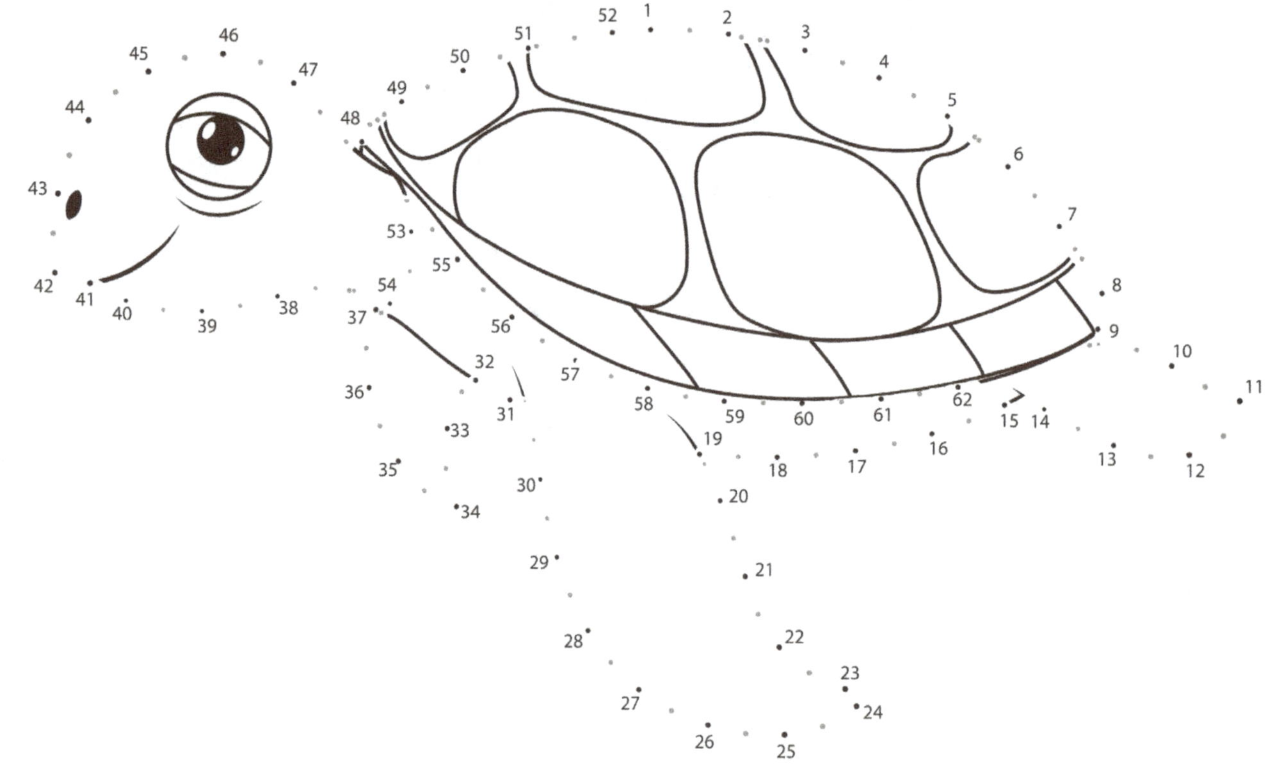

Turtle

Frog

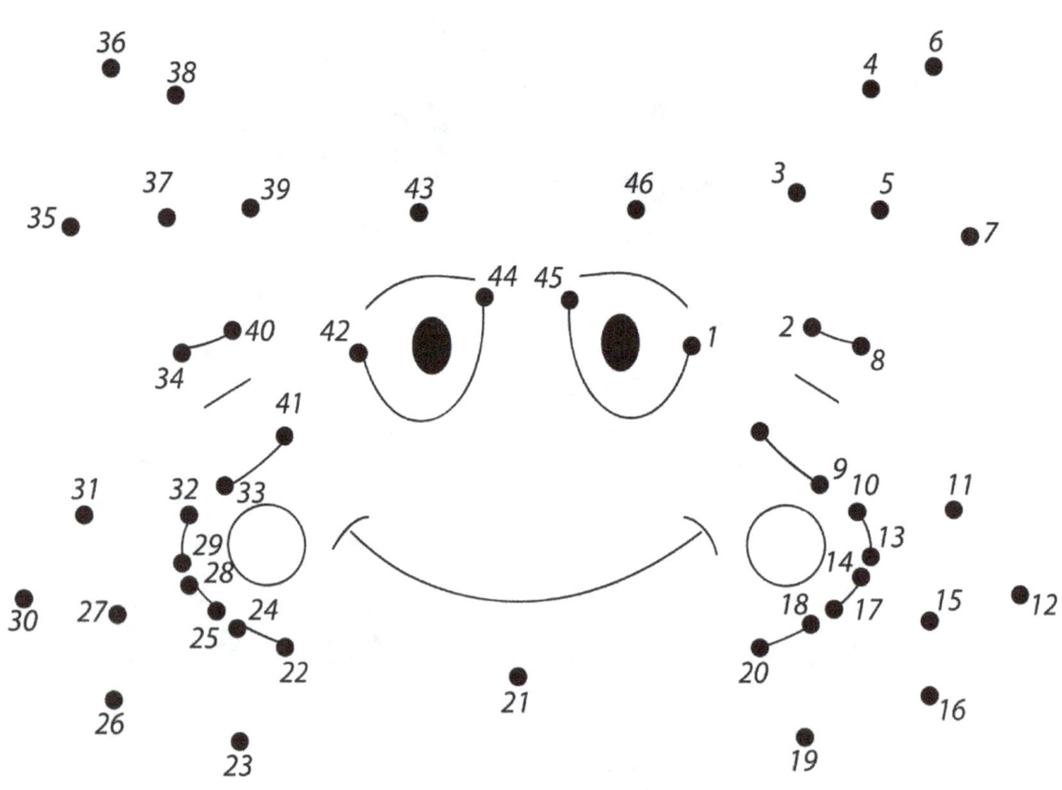

Crab

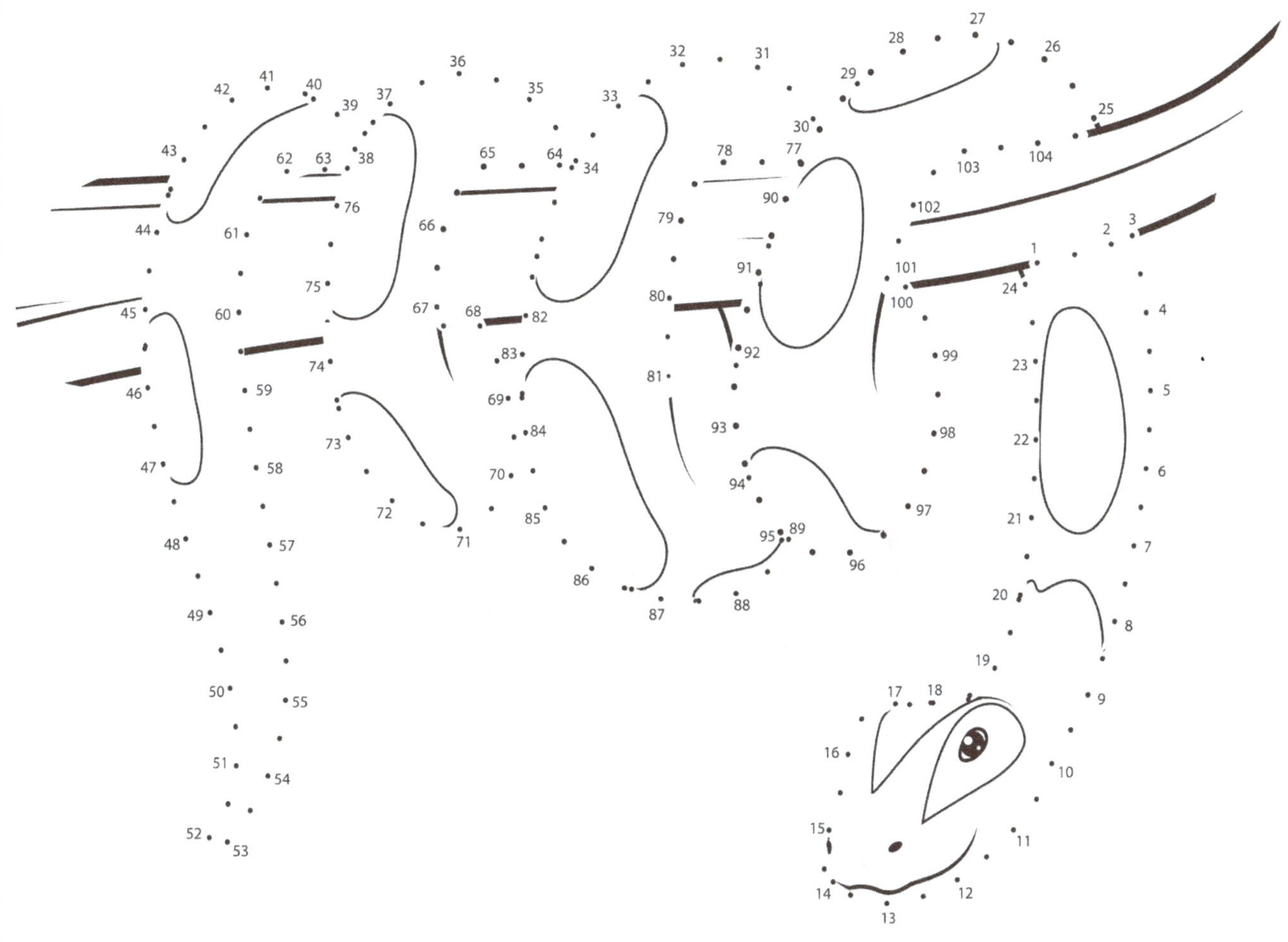

Snake

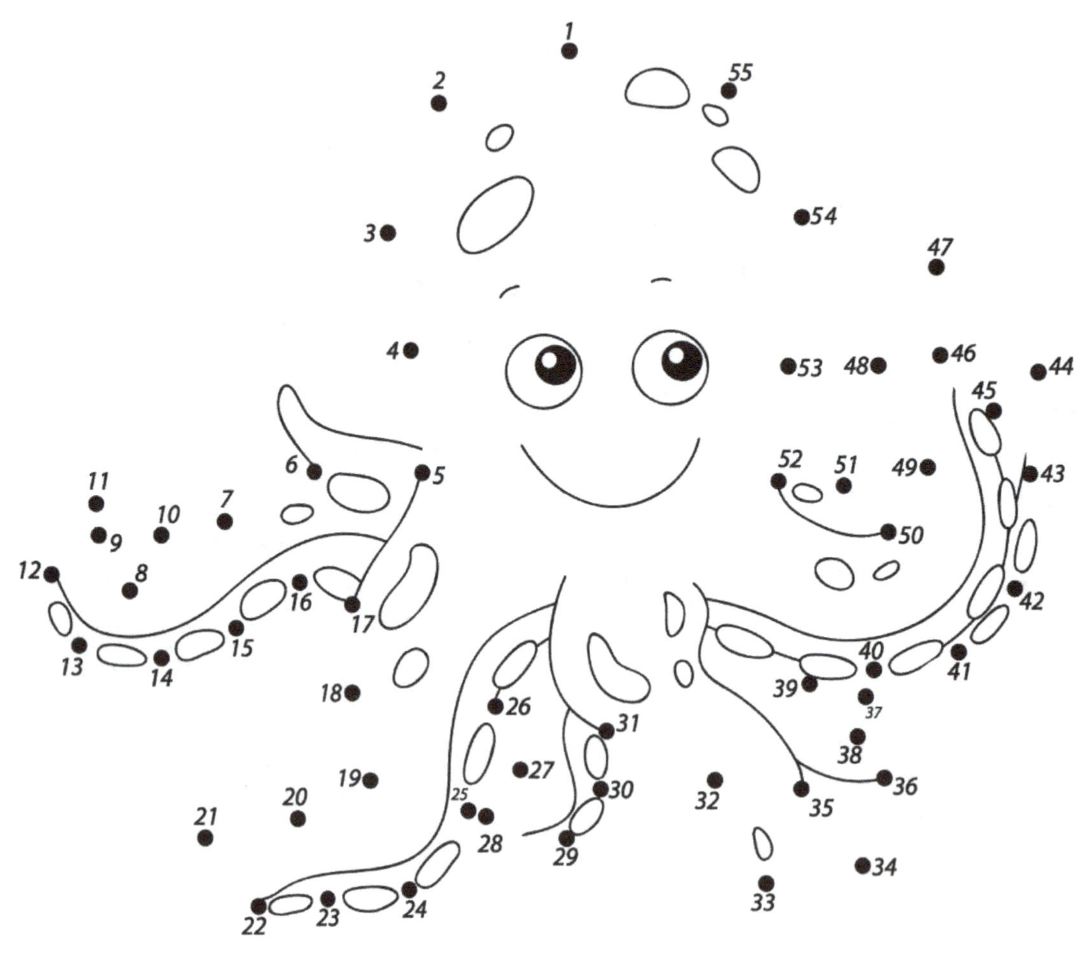

Octopus

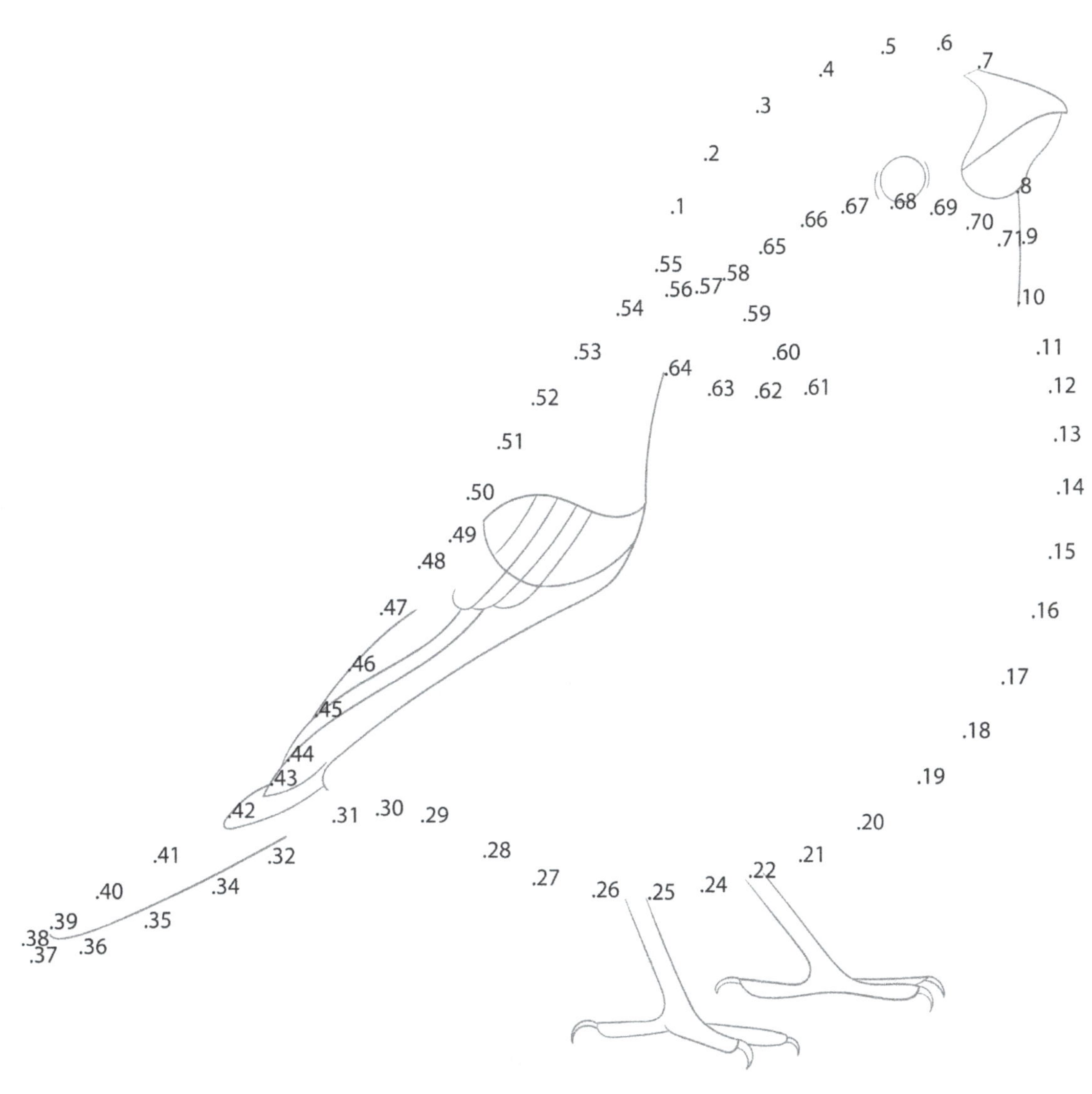

Bird

Penguin

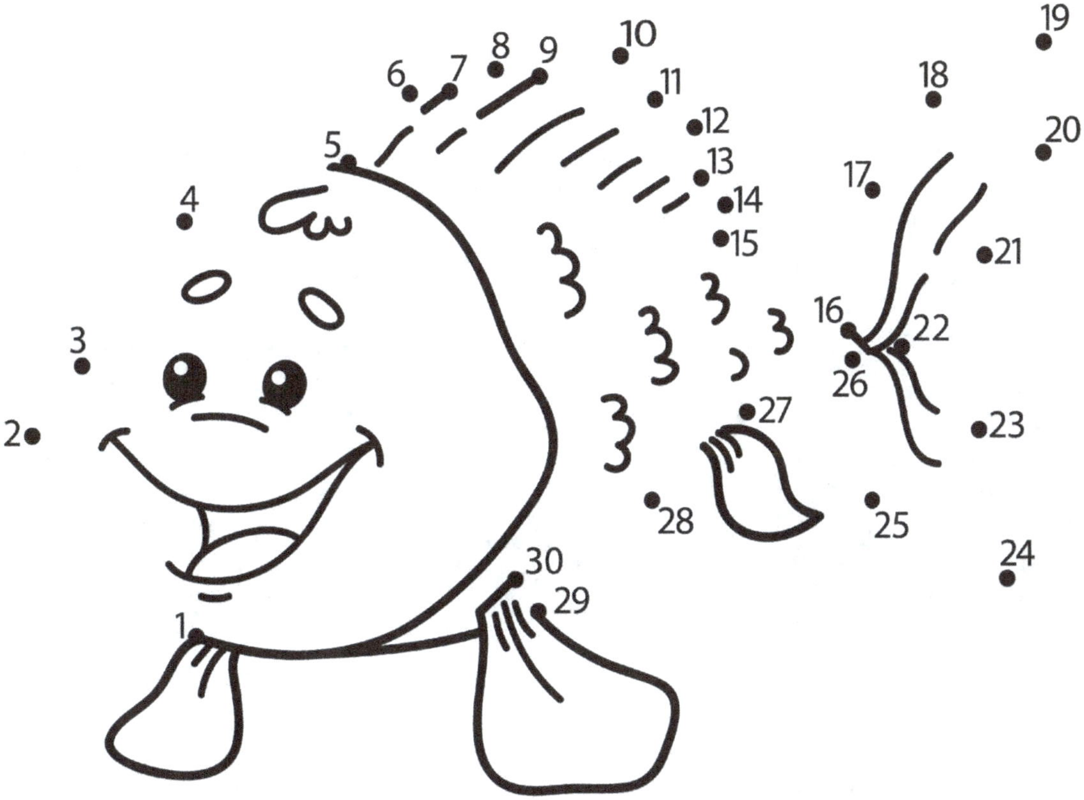
1
2
3
4
5
6
7
8
9
10
11
12
13
14
15
16
17
18
19
20
21
22
23
24
25
26
27
28
29
30

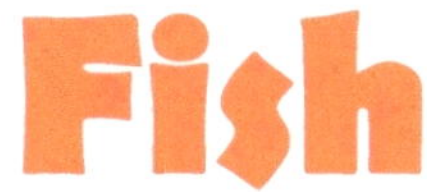

Fish

Visit

BABY PROFESSOR
EDUCATION KIDS

www.BabyProfessorBooks.com

to download Free Baby Professor eBooks
and view our catalog of new and exciting
Children's Books